The Thumb Rules of Ideation and Project Management

About Authors: Guy Kawasaki is #1 Management Consultant of the World —and our team of authors is #2 consultant of the World. They have consulted more than 2000 companies in the start-up space and had dealt with more than 18000 companies for product launch, business strategy, marketing strategy, and business process re-engineering and change management. They have copyright for some core management principles like #14Sooktas© #recruitmentherd© #tencust© #beerlaunch© #sagstick©.#selectiverejection© They can be consulted at: www.kalkie.org

Our client list includes:

1. *Det Norske Veritas*
2. *Suzlon Energy*
3. *Green Energy*
4. *Kirloskar Cummins*
5. *Google (email confirmation awaited)*
6. *Reliance Industries*
7. *Grasim*
8. *Adani Wilmar*
9. *Cooperative Bank of India*

Prologue:

Smart people delegate work, whereas fools try to do work on their own with bunch of jokers. Your father and mother are your best teacher –

as they teach you perseverance, diligence, spend-thrift and discipline. You can learn from their mistakes. Your mother teaches you —how to raise your family and your father teaches how to cope up with the hardships of your life. This is true for team management. Your team leader is like your father and your mother is like HR Manager. Respect and Love your Parents- and you will learn how to run a business. Taking a cue from Cyrus Mistry —Tata feud, we think that family run business is the best business, as stake holders are bonded in a relationship. The external employee can quit company anytime — but family members, even if illiterate or under- performing, knows that a penny earned for the company will have at least $0.001 for him. The PTC sites of the world were creation of a con- artist of our team, who thought that earning 2 *cents a day would teach him discipline and value of money.*

Please follow us on Twitter @rajmehatalb

And Subscribe to our YouTube Channel:
https://www.youtube.com/channel/UCxd4UCONGTM63ii4edmK1rA

Visit us at: www.kalkie.org, www.igurucool.in, www.kalkie.in *for more books*

Explore working with us at:
http://www.igurucool.in/earn.html

Chapters

1. Hopeless Romantic

Chapter One: Hopeless Romantic

I am biggest devout of Lord Shiva. Shiva means auspicious, pure, saumya, smooth. Lord Shiva is the biggest Management Guru ever born. He always has perfect plan –and works with clock-work precision. No one emulate him. Whereas I pick pieces from multiple sources to launch a grand assault. I have 25 sources of revenue and in worst case scenario too I make 17 grand per month working from home.

This was my revenue target 11 years back, but I am glad that I reached there. I challenged few students –who were making 150K per month that 17 grand per month consistently is better than 150K per month. Then they mocked at me, and now they are struggling even for 10K per month.

I am hopeless romantic, I believe in fairy tales. I am in love with love. One of my prospective employers making $1 Million per year offered me a very high paying job –I mocked at him for two things: First on his dismal revenue figures, and secondly on his anger of North American companies –who were eroding his client base. He was charging Rupees 30K/per year, per terminal from BPO companies.

That was the first time I got deep insight into flawed business models. Charging 30K for software installed in a computer worth 24K, does not make sense. After that I did research on many successful companies, and many failed business models.

Then I concluded that the best business model is low cost and high volume. Consumers are generally poor. They prefer low priced highly satisfactory items. Price is the biggest barrier for many consumers.

Business is like getting girls in your life. A guy gets attracted to every beautiful girl –but at the end it matters –how many girls he wins. If you closely analyze the girl –and see her deeply –then you will find that some girls are not meant for you. Only few girls are meant for you. The most common reason for rejection of girl is that you would feel toothpaste in her mouth, or there is some stink emanating from her body.

We have a very solid business model for home-based businesses. Please visit http://www.igurucool.in/earn.html

**

Chapter Two: The need to start a Business

There are six reasons to start a business:

1. To wish to be stinking rich
2. To emulate Bill Gates, Larry Page or Sergey Brin
3. To marry sexiest girl alive
4. To fight unemployment
5. To serve the society
6. To fulfill all the above

There is no doubt that Kate Middleton –the Queen of England is the sexiest girl alive, and to fulfill points 1 and 2 are very difficult. So most people start business to fulfill point 4, 5. Starting a business gives you sense of ownership and satisfaction. It helps you to reach your personal goals. The personal goals of almost all individuals are:

1. Get four square meal
2. Get a shelter
3. Pay the monthly bills
4. Entertain the family
5. Save for the future
6. Educate the kids
7. Help pets and poor people

8. Earn respect in society.

Most of the people look for jobs to achieve these objectives, but there are lots of road-blocks to it. I just glanced through a tweet in twitter that 4,65,000 people in United States had stopped looking for jobs –before the 2016 US Presidential Elections. The reason is obvious – they might have been rejected multiple times by the companies. Now they might have no option except to launch their own startup. A few ideas for startups would be:

1. Web-Design
2. Helping the lawyers
3. Voice-over and translation
4. Starting their counseling center
5. Teach kids through Internet
6. Work remotely as consultant
7. Write Books
8. Launch a band

So this is the genesis of the start-up. Necessity is mother of all inventions. Big advertising spaces like Google and Facebook are suffocating the free-spirit of entrepreneurs by illogical policies, so through this book –I urge them to bear with these novices –as they do not know the simplest thing –how to write an Advertisement.

Internet has become a big differentiator –and with a small team of 4-5 people, you can have a successful SOHO (Small Office, Home Office). We have a very solid business model for home-based businesses. Please visit http://www.igurucool.in/earn.html

**

Chapter Three: Funding Options

Now I have a simple principle for uplifting society. All those people who have net worth more than $1 Million – should start garage venture and start his/her own firm – working for other companies. This is applicable for people who live in independent villa –those living in flats should not try it.

Then these people would be absorbed in the venture – and the entrepreneur should start expanding his/her business. Now an iteration of this would be –the people employed would start their own venture –when their net-worth crosses $1 Million. Thus a big-bang would entrepreneurship would be unleashed.

Now I have request with real-estate developers –do not invest in flats; invest in low-cost villas -because flats are very prone to earthquake, sexual abuse and apathy towards elderly people.

**

Now let us discuss funding options. Say a big no venture capital firms. Collect cash from friends, relatives, banks or through crowd-funding.

Again say no to crowd-funding sites. Make a video – advertise on YouTube, and collect cash through PayPal on your website. Advertise your website through AdWords and Twitter and collect cash on your website. Maintain an excel sheet and allocate shares to all your investors.

Never prepare for big launch. Slow and modest start –is needed.

**

Please follow us on Twitter @rajmehatalb

And Subscribe to our YouTube Channel:
[*https://www.youtube.com/channel/UCxd4UCONGTM63ii4edmK1rA*](https://www.youtube.com/channel/UCxd4UCONGTM63ii4edmK1rA)

Chapter Four: Big Projects from Big Companies

Sharing from our personal experience, we started a software company in Bangalore in 2006. To be precise – in May 2006. We had good domain knowledge and we were operating from a small apartment. Our main tasks were:

- Website Design
- Search Engine Optimization
- Manpower Consulting
- Developing Small Software for SMEs
- Digital Marketing
- Content Writing

- Management Consulting
- Human Resource Consulting

We generated leads mostly through email database and website of vendors. We also got leads from Google Adwords and Directory Maximizer. Some of our keywords were on #1 position of search engines, and we got some business from there.

Our main income was from content writing and developing small software for clients in Java and Visual Basic. It took typically three days to develop a $1000 software. We were making $150K annually and had nearly 500K visitors to our site monthly.

Then we got a big client from USA, it was a multi-million mortgage company and we got a $800K order, which we completed in 3 months.

After that we starting joking about INFY, TC, and Geom. The buzz created by us got a big buyer and we sold our company for nearly $11 Million. A part of money was paid, and another part never paid. A court case is still pending in Bangalore. The company which we sold is now listed company with more than $650 Million in annual revenue.

After that we started a BPO in Greater Noida and sank all our money trusting a big Financial Services Company in USA –which revoked its contract.

So the moral of the story is –trust big clients if they are paying you for small utilization of your resources, but never trust a big client if it is utilizing lot of your resources. We have a very solid business model for home-based businesses. Please visit http://www.igurucool.in/earn.html

**

Chapter Five: Down to Dust

Whenever you get a project, proper planning is needed. You should prepare a flowchart for every stage of project, allocate resource, do budget analysis, test the prototype and calculate the profitability. If there is no profitability then become generous enough to reject the project –no matter how big the client is. Losses are compounding. Strings of losses can sink your company and make you bankrupt.

A few examples of loss making companies, where our small investments are involved:

- Pepperfry
- Angel Broking
- Tinyowl
- Zomato
- Archid Ply

We are optimistic that even these companies are not profitable, and then with our backup plan we can recover 2x of our investments.

One of our investments doing really good is Frankfinn Airhostess Academy –both moneywise and beautiful girl wise. A lot of our employees have Punjabi Airhostess as their girlfriend. The Sardarji owner of the company tried to launch Frankfinn Music, and it failed –thank God that we did not invest in that company.

**

The 19 stages of project management are:

1. Contacting the client
2. Getting the order
3. Signing the contract
4. Getting RFP
5. Getting RPA
6. Brainstorming with Team
7. Resource Allocation
8. Selecting Team Lead
9. Doing Cost Analysis
10.   Setting Deadlines
11.   Showing Sample to Client
12.   Getting Clients Approval
13.   Starting the Work
14.   Developing Prototype
15.   Beta Testing
16.   Getting Clients Signoff
17.   Developing Full Product
18.   Getting Clients Signoff
19.   Getting Paid

**

Chapter Six: Project Management

Now let us talk about project management in detail. Components of the Project Plan Include:

1. Baselines. Baselines are called performance measures, as the performance of the entire project is measured against them. They are the project's three approved points and include: scope, schedule, and cost baselines. There are important Baseline management plans. These plans include documentation -how variances to the baselines will be handled in the project. Project baseline need to be reviewed and managed. This might entail additional planning, with the effect that the baseline(s) might change. What project team will do when variances to the baselines occur, including new process followed, who will be notified, how the changes will be funded?

Planning process includes a risk management plan, a staffing plan, a quality plan, a procurement plan, and a communications plan.

2. Define roles and responsibilities. Not all key stakeholders will review all documents, so it is necessary

to determine who on the project needs to approve which parts of the plan. Some of the key players are:

- Project sponsor, who owns and funds the entire project,
- Project team, who build the end product.
- Others, such as auditors, quality and risk analysts, procurement specialists, and so on may also participate on the project. They may need to approve the parts that pertain to them, such as the Quality or Procurement plan.

3. Hold a kickoff meeting.

Some of the topics that might be included in a kickoff meeting:

- Business vision and strategy
- Project vision
- Roles and responsibilities
- Team commitments
- How team makes decisions
- Ground rules
- Team building

4. Develop a Scope Statement. The Scope Statement should include:

- Business need and business problem
- Project objectives
- Benefits of completing the project
- Project deliverables
- Key milestones and the approach

5. Develop scope baseline. This deliverable WBS forms the scope baseline. It identifies all the deliverables produced on the project. Takes large deliverables and breaks them into a hierarchy of smaller deliverables. Small deliverables are called "work packages"

6. Develop the schedule and cost baselines. Here:

- Identify activities and tasks of the work packages, creating a WBS of tasks.
- Identify resources for each task.
- Estimate how long it will take for task.
- Estimate cost of each task, and hourly rate of team members.

- Consider how much time each resource can devote to project.
- Determine interdependent tasks and develop critical path.
- Develop schedule of all the tasks and estimates.
- Develop the cost baseline.

7. Create baseline management plans.

8. Develop the staffing plan.

9. Analyze project quality and risks.

10. Communicate with Stake Holders

**

Chapter Seven: Life-Cycles of Project

Now let us discuss how the project is executed. You can start from home. We have a very solid business model for home-based businesses. Please visit http://www.igurucool.in/earn.html Try some projects individually, then with a team, and then scale up.

The various phases are included in five phases. Now let us discuss them:

5 Basic Phases of Project Management

The Project Management Institute (PMI) defined project management as "the application of knowledge, skills, tools and techniques to a broad range of activities in order to meet the requirements of a particular project." The process of directing and controlling a project from start to finish may be further divided into 5 basic phases:

1. Project ideation and initiation

An idea for a project is carefully examined to determine whether or not it is beneficial for organization. During this
phase, a decision making team identifies if the project can realistically be completed.

2. Project definition and planning

A project plan, project charter and/or project scope may be put in writing, outlining the work to be performed. During this phase, a team should prioritize the project, calculate a budget and schedule, and determine what resources are needed.

3. Project launch or execution

Resources' tasks are distributed and teams are informed of their responsibilities. This is the ideal time to bring up important project related information.

4. Project performance and control

Project managers will compare project status and monitor progress to the actual plan, as resources perform the delegated work. During this phase, project managers often adjust schedules or do what is necessary to keep the project meeting the targets and deadlines.

5. Project close

After project tasks are completed and the client has approves the beta outcome, the iteration is done to do the final deliverables. An evaluation is needed to highlight project success and archive finds from project history.

Projects and project management processes vary from sectors to industry; however, these are universal methods of a project. The goal is typically to offer a product, change a business process or to solve a problem in order to benefit the organization.

**

Chapter Eight: Controlled Testing

In India, many engineers build bridges that are washed away by water. Many contractors build roads which develop potholes within a year. There are softwares which starts crashing from day one. So there are lots of job related with software testing.

The basic principles of testing are same. You go on the path as per your knowledge. Keep exploring better options, and keep modifying the product until it gets near perfection. Test the beta version with the client, if he says ok then release it to relatively large audience. They will find flaws and the loop-holes that do not work for large users. Modify the product, get final signoff from the client, and then go for mass release.

Keep coming up with updates after every few months.

**

Chapter Nine: To Dump or to Launch

There are many failed products like housing.com, whatsapp, orkut etc which brought dismal revenue to creator. The expenses involved in running the product were multiple times higher than revenue. I read somewhere that whatsapp was acquired in $19 billion, but revenue from whatsapp was mere $40 million. Orkut was shut down and housing.com is in disarray.

It is a sensible business decision to withdraw the product if it is not profitable, or find means to make it profitable. It is important that a product is profitable; if not then find means to make it profitable.

No business is better than bad business. Imagine the cost of servers and wages of employees who are maintaining whatsapp.

It is general trend in software industry that if a product has high numbers of members, then acquire it at high price. But the analysts should look at the fact that how much revenue those members are giving to the company.

**

A highly rated ecommerce company in India has very high number of members, but it is running at annual loss of Rupees 2000 crore. One should think –from where this additional Rupees 2000 crore is coming.

**

We have a very solid business model for home-based businesses. Please visit http://www.igurucool.in/earn.html

Chapter Ten: Case Studies

In this chapter we would take up the case of two products: Maggi from Nestle and Dantkanti tooth powder from Baba Ramdev.

In the 1980s, the world economy was changing. People were gearing up for fast paced life. Instant food was the need of hour. People wanted emergency food, so nestle launched Maggi –so that people can have both taste and convenience. In India Maggi was launched through the school kids, and then it made to heart of elders.

It was a perfect product at low price.

Indians are orthodox, and especially elder people wanted something which is good and at low price. Baba Ramdev found an opportunity in it and launched Dantkanti, an ayurvedic product at a price 20-30% lower than normal tooth paste and product became a good hit.

**

End of Book